T0077987

A Songbook

A Book of Lyrics and Poems

JOANN LOGAN RATHJE

Copyright © 2021 JoAnn Logan Rathje.

All rights reserved. No part of this book may be used or reproduced by any means, graphic, electronic, or mechanical, including photocopying, recording, taping or by any information storage retrieval system without the written permission of the author except in the case of brief quotations embodied in critical articles and reviews.

Archway Publishing books may be ordered through booksellers or by contacting:

Archway Publishing
1663 Liberty Drive
Bloomington, IN 47403
www.archwaypublishing.com
844-669-3957

Because of the dynamic nature of the Internet, any web addresses or links contained in this book may have changed since publication and may no longer be valid. The views expressed in this work are solely those of the author and do not necessarily reflect the views of the publisher, and the publisher hereby disclaims any responsibility for them.

Any people depicted in stock imagery provided by Getty Images are models, and such images are being used for illustrative purposes only. Certain stock imagery © Getty Images.

ISBN: 978-1-6657-0939-2 (sc)
ISBN: 978-1-6657-0940-8 (e)

Library of Congress Control Number: 2021914071

Print information available on the last page.

Archway Publishing rev. date: 09/17/2021

SLIM

A

The skin on slim is lean and trim

He's so popular with the ladies

Cause he dr

ives a red Mercedes

He gets stoned and high

In the nighttime sky

Dancing in the moonlight

Well into the night

At party time

A

He likes a girl

with blonde pin curls

She wears high heels

It makes his world reel

And his eyes peel

Her want for Slim

She soon reveals

They took a chance

And in a glance

They found romance

They were amazed

And they felt crazed

They kissed themselves into a trance

And they made love in a dance

I REMEMBER YOU

A

Lilly of the valley

And violets bloom

In the titter tauter days my youth

Taking pictures of ourselves at Kreski's

In the photo both

Ping pong in the basement

And valley ball in the back yard

Summer time spent exchanging baseball cards

That came with the bubble gum

We had so much fun

We played cops and robbers

And we did run and run

B

I remember you

I remember you

I remember you

Do you remember me too?

A

Christmas Eve night the church stood still

Silently upon a hill

Someone threw a brick through the stain glass

This made the preacher man mad so mad

He swept up the fragments of glass

And put them in a can of trash

That stood on the grass

It was so bad

And it made us so sad

B

I got lost in a maze

We had to go our separate ways

But here was no closure

Our friendship wasn't over

Sad raindrops on my window sill

I remember you still

And always will

Forever and until

The end of my world

B

FOR THE THRILLS

I loved you for the thrills

My lace and frills

I have your picture framed in lapis lazuli

It reminds me of our past dreams

The way we use to scheme our happenings

Of diamond rings and things

We could sit here and play all day

That's what you use to say

My love for you I hid as if I was just a kid

And I'll remember you when I wake in the morning

and in my dreams at night

My love for you I hid as if I was just a kid

And I'll remember you in the morning

And in my dreams at night

Today on NBC

B

It's *Today* on NBC.

It's *Today* on NBC.

It's *Today*!

Our way!

It's *Today* on NBC.

A

Making my bed

With Hoda and Savannah.

Dylan is her

Very cute self today.

Al Roker is visiting

With everyone in the rain.

C

On *Today*!

On *Today*.

On *Today*.

A

Getting in on the country's weather scene.

Watching Minnesota's KARE 11 team.

Kristen is high up on the beam.

Starting the day with *Today* is my way.

Listening and looking on *Today*.

D

On *Today*!

On *Today*!

On *Today*!

B

Kristen does an analogy.

Today has a friend in me,

Devoted until eternity.

Today has a friend in me.

Peter has an inspirational football team.

Today has a friend in me.

B

Now it's Wayfair, and I don't care.

Otezla, you make people's skin rare and fair.

Steals and deals and smartwatches everywhere.

People watching from Rockefeller Center's frozen rink.

Now Donald Trump is on the brink.

A

Friday *Night Heights* is very calm.

Corona coming from my yawns

Jet stream making snow in the East,

Making for a white Christmas feast.

Weekend Today and all week long,

I watch on my backyard skating pond.

Snow for all of us today and beyond.

Now what will that be on?

Educational and informational is on too,

So, I can see what's going on with you.

Now I can go outside and enjoy my day.

Today made inspirational

In so many ways.

B

In Another Place in Time

A

Sitting around on my brown leather couch,

It hurts my back and butt so much.

I try calling you on my telephone.

I know you're home,

You're just not picking up.

It hurts so much,

And it's the biggest cut.

Now I know I'll never see you again,

Not your handsome dark eyes and hair.

I'm out of luck.

Now I'll sleep all alone

In a home we used to share.

When we met on the dating site,

You were the sweetest one I found.

When I lost you, I put up a fight

Because you didn't want me around.

A

Now you're gone, and there's no one new.

Didn't want our romance to be through.

I can't meet anyone like you again.

I've tried to make new friends.

Losing you is the worst that's ever been.

But I will remember those summer winds.

They blew through my long blonde hair.

The winds I used to ride on and fly on

When I ran right by your side

In another place in another time

With the love we had to share.

I'm just so sorry you don't care.

Wish our romance could be spared.

B

In another place in time,

I'll find you again

And make you mine.

We'll be more than just friends

In another place in time.

Life Continues on and Around

B

Life continues on and around.

People come, and people go.

We could have been tender then,

When was not such a long time ago.

A

We're not starting over again?

Can we just be friends?

I can't believe it's the end.

It's the end of me, us, and mine.

I will want you till the end of time.

Our life together was so fine,

We'll be together in infinite time.

C

Now you're dumping me at the altar.

Yeah! Yeah!

Dumping me at the altar, sweetie.

Yeah! Yeah!

Dumping me at the altar, sweetie.

A

Now you're leaving, my sweet?

Can't our romance repeat?

A new romance at your feet?

I can no longer compete?

Your new adore can't be beat.

Red roses once smelled so sweet.

C

Roller-coaster passionate ride,

Getting the ups and downs.

Now you've given me a long, wide frown.

B

C

Now you're dumping me at the altar, sweetie.

Dumping me at the altar.

Yeah! Yeah!

Dumping me at the altar.

Yeah! Yeah!

B

Life continues on and around.

People come, and people go.

We could have been in tender then.

When was not such a long time ago.

Can We Be Friends?

B

Can I see you again?

I want to be your friend.

You're the best that's come my way.

Today you've made my day.

You make me so hap, hap, happy.

A

You make me feel so bashful.

Your fine physique

Makes you quite dishful.

We met in rainy April.

We went out on a romp.

Our tender dance can't stop.

B

A

You're number one in a majority.

You are my piano prodigy.

My love for you is as sweet as pink taffy.

I want you more than butterscotch candy.

B

A

My ship without you is

As lonely as the desert sun.

Without your desire,

I'll come undone.

Without your devotion,

I'm as frightened

As a cornered cat.

With your devotion,

I'm as optimistic as

A college graduate.

I have all the love for you

As I once had for

My mother's long, loving hands.

Without your love

I'm a one-woman marching band.

Without you by me

I can get as desperate

As a desert without sunshine.

You're my best friend of mine.

A

Without you I'm as whimsically cool

As a Greenland ice cap.

My devotion is as fast

As the roadrunner.

Can't go on without you,

So, let's get down to it.

A

You're as fumingly hot

As a blackened skillet.

Your adoration is softer than

A puffy white cloud

On a summer's sunny day.

With your adoration,

I have enough energy

To run a marathon

On some bleak and rainy

Sunless Sunday in May.

B

Ashamed

A

I don't need to feel so ashamed.

Stop shaming me.

No shaming me,

Not blaming me.

Under the ground I hid;

I know what I did.

I had too much energy.

I have no memory.

A

Do I need to be shunned?

My punishment is the one thing

That got me undone.

All my anger is gone.

Won't speak to my friend again,

Enabling me till the end.

A

Whatever I did,

I was only following his lead.

Please don't make me bleed.

I'm off of that speed.

A

I don't need to be so ashamed.

Please don't shame me.

I don't need to be so ashamed.

Stop shaming me.

Not blaming me,

No shaming me.

No, not blaming me.

Blue Bed

A

I left him when he left me for dead,

Went back to my mama's home.

Then I was all alone.

Cause I knew I couldn't make it on my own.

It was so nice just to lay my head

Where my mama kept my own blue bed.

When I left him when he left me for dead,

Blue sheets, sash, and pillows were where I lay my head.

A

I was back in my old blue bed

In my mama's home, now all alone

Cause I couldn't make it on my own.

So good to be back in my old room

And back in my own blue bed,

Blue sheets and sash and pillows for my blue head

When I left him when he left me for dead

.

He's a Cad Guitarist

Their sexual misbehavior—

He's a suicide driver,

She's a suicide rider.

He's a rogue musician,

Such rogue musician.

He's a cad guitarist,

Such a cad guitarist.

How many times

Did she lose her spirit?

Could she hear it,

The thunder clapping?

She lost her spirit.

The earth is snapping

Because of their offensive sex behavior.

He's a suicide driver,

She's a suicide rider.

She did everything

That he wanted

So, she could please him

And give him pleasure.

A want so grim,

So, he could measure

Her affection,

A wrong connection.

He made her find out

Just what he wanted.

She was devout

To give him pleasure.

He had allure.

She never heard of

The things he wanted.

She told him as she shrove,

But she was unwanted.

But she found out

In a way most devout.

Just to please him

And on a whim,

He took her up,

And he said, "Yup,"

Then he lost his fuse.

She was his muse,

Then he lied to her.

He disrespected her,

Rejected her,

Ignored her

When she needed him the most.

How many times

Had he ruined her adoration?

He wounded her adulation?

He used her affection?

She went through a trauma;

It was a huge drama,

And he wasn't there.

Playing truth or dare

He wouldn't speak to her

Because he didn't care.

It didn't feel right,

So, she killed herself out of spite.

No, he just came and went

And left her spent,

And only a few days passed.

When she died,

There was no place he could hide.

The pain she went through

He would never know;

He could never come close.

He would be there for her

When she needed him most.

He was just a rogue musician,

Such a rogue musician.

He was a cad guitarist,

Just a cad guitarist.

How many times

Did he rob her soul?

Did he steal her spirit?

He killed her

And her adulation

Like a thief in the night.

She cared for him

With all of her might.

She trusted in him

And died in spite

In the heat of the night.

But to him it,

It didn't feel right.

He was a rogue musician,

Such a rogue musician.

He was a cad guitarist,

Such a sad guitarist,

A cad guitarist.

How many times

Did he steal her soul?

Did he kill her spirit?

He took all her strength away.

And then she killed herself one day.

He killed her adulation.

He robbed her of her admiration.

She lost his affection

And took her life

To be freed from her strife.

She lost the man she loved and adored.

She couldn't feel her pain anymore.

I'm Never Coming Back Home

I left you a long time ago,

and I'm never coming back home

Because of all your manic episodes

and all your crazy calls.

I got all the messages

that you left

me on my telephone.

You swept me off my feet,

and I never claimed defeat.

But you have to take the heat.

You even called me a little creep.

I left you a long time ago,

and I never want to come home

because of all your manic episodes

and all your nutty calls.

I got all the messages

that you left me

on my telephone.

And I'm never, never, never, coming back home.

Cage Fighter

B

I'm a cage fighter

and I'm punched drunk

and I am a punk.

I'm a cage fighter

and I'm punched drunk

and I am a punk.

A

They tear me lose,

and I kill like a noose

I go off like a fuse.

I'm as mean as a jackal.

Did you hear me crackle?

Hear me crackle.

Crackle,

Crackle.

B

A

One jab to the right,

A fist and a fight.

I'm fast and I'm furious.

And aren't you curious?

You curious?

Curious?

Curious?

B

You Caused Me Pain

You hurt me and caused me pain.

All the mixed emotions,

All the guilt and shame.

So many stupid games that you played.

I really wish you well because

I forgave you for all the hell that you caused.

I shouldn't have, but I did,

So, I could move on, and I could give

To all the others who are pain

And still suffer today

From all their anger,

Their mixed emotions,

All the guilt and shame,

When you hurt me,

And we played your stupid games.

You killed my innocence and stole my identity away.

I felt ashamed because you drugged me

And left me insane.

And then I took all the blame.

Summertime

Butterflies fly around the trees and flowers

In the heat of the summertime.

Sunny days and dusky nights,

Sweet pretty butterflies fly

In the heat of the summertime.

I can fly like butterflies' fly,

Those sweet, pretty butterflies that fly

In the hottest of days,

The long days of summer.

In sunniest of days

and the dusks of nighttime,

Butterflies fly all the days of summertime.

Sweet and colorful butterflies flying

In the hottest of days.

And in the warm night skies of summertime,

Bumblebees fly from flower to flower

To drink their nectar.

I can fly like bumblebees fly

To and from flowers that shine

In the splendid assort hues,

Pastel and bright colors,

So true they produce

the skinny, smooth yellow glow

And the sweetest of honey.

So true do bumble bees fly,

Creating large honeycombs

From the flowers they drank nectar.

I like to watch hummingbirds fly.

I can fly like hummingbirds fly,

Fluttering their wings that thumber.

So fast do their wings take flight,

Those hummingbird wings flitter

At lightning speeds.

In the heat of summer

I will take flight

In the darkness of night

With the moon that glows.

In my secret sweet dreams

Of this summer,

In the hot days

Of my August days

Of my youth.

He's a Cheater

He's a cheater,

He's a mistreater,

He's a deceiver.

He's afraid of losing her.

He sees other women on the side,

And he won't tell nothing but lies.

But he's never satisfied;

He's reckless, selfish, and mean.

And other women that he sees,

Well, he says that

"They don't mean a thing."

And his woman,

she doesn't

suspect a thing,

And she believes

that he's loyal.

But he's nothing

like that at all.

He's a cheater,

He a mistreater,

He's a deceiver.

And he's afraid of losing her.

And he's sees

other women

on the side.

And he can't tell

nothing but lies.

And he's never satisfied.

He's a cheater,

He's a mistreater,

He's a deceiver.

I Won't Listen

I won't listen to what people tell me about sex.

I won't listen to what people tell me about sex.

They don't know what normal is.

They don't know what normal is.

Everyone is different.

Everyone is different.

He can't hurt me anymore.

He can't hurt me anymore.

I can relax and let go.

I can relax and let go.

I'm Singing Songs of Love

I'm singing songs of love, but not for me.

So many songs of love, but not for me.

And though I can't resist the beauty of your kiss,

I'm still singing songs of love, but not for me.

You think so highly of yourself, I see.

So egocentric, and yet most would agree

You're narcissistic, yes, and yet I can see.

A

I'm singing songs of love, but not for me.

So many songs of love, but not for me.

And though I can't resist the loveliness of your kiss,

I'm singing songs of love, but not for me.

You really did all you could to take advantage of me.

And I'm the sweetest one you'll ever meet.

You really took full advantage of me.

And though I can't resist the exquisiteness of our kiss,

I'm singing songs of love, but not for me.

B

Dating Apps

Who's on Ok Cupid?

Who's on Ok Stoopid?

Who's on Ok Cupid?

Who's on Ok Stoopid?

Who am I sexting now?

Who's my biggest flirt?

Who can I get to know?

Who can I kiss?

Who will I miss?

Who can I date?

Who could I wed?

Who will be my friend?

And love me till the end?

Love me till I'm dead?

Who's on Ok Cupid?

Who's on Ok Stoopid?

Who's on Ok Cupid?

Who's on Ok Stoopid?

Princess Warrior

My sister Patsy,

My sister Patsy,

Well, she just couldn't see

Just how bad she was to me,

Now she's cold

And dead

And under

And I'm

her Princess Warrior.

I'm her Princess Warrior.

Princess Warrior,

Princess Warrior,

Warrior,

Warrior.

Untouchable

A

I'm untouchable,

I'm untouchable.

I'm too shy,

I'm too scared,

I'm too sick,

I'm too old,

I'm too had.

I'm too sore,

And I'm too bad.

I'm too crazy,

And I'm too drab.

I'm untouchable.

I'm untouchable,

A

He's untouchable,

He's untouchable.

He's too young,

And he's too old.

He's too busy,

And he's too cold.

He's too late,

And he's too stoned.

He's too creepy,

And he's all bones.

We're untouchable,

We're untouchable.

Be My Baby

Hello, baby.

How's life treating you?

I'm a fright without makeup.

Need my lipstick

And mascara,

Etcetera.

Hello, baby.

How you feeling?

Miss you sweety.

Want to swoon you.

Want you, honey,

Need you by me,

Etcetera.

Can we kiss

And get to it?

Miss you, baby.

We're not through yet.

Don't leave me

Until I'm finished.

Bye now, honey.

Nice to see you.

Kiss me baby.

Sending my love.

You send me darlin'.

Give me a hug.

Be my honey.

Is that enough?

Eating Disorder

B

Doc, won't you help me please?

I got an eating disorder;

Can't get enough food to order.

I got an eating disorder,

I got an eating disorder.

A

Roller-coaster weight

Weighing me up and down.

It all gave me

A big bad frown.

Can't fit into my clothes.

My problem is so gross.

I want my stomach flat,

But it needs

A big fat hat.

Did a thousand sit ups

Night and day.

But it won't take

My stomach away.

B

A

B

I started wearing tunics

And plus-size clothes.

The problem got me so engrossed.

I went on fad diets galore,

But I couldn't stop eating more and more.

It was never diagnosed.

The problem was so morose.

B

Went from skinny and thin

Too big and fat;

I couldn't win.

Roller-coaster weight

Weighing me up and down.

It all gave me one big frown,

And I felt like such a clown.

B

Gotta Have a Lover

You got to have a lover

like my lover.

There's no other lover

like my lover.

You got to have a baby like my baby.

You never had a baby—

and I don't mean maybe—

like my baby.

You got to have a honey like my honey.

There's no other honey like my honey.

You got to have a sweet like my sweety.

There's no other sweety like my sweety.

You got to have a lover like my lover.

There's no lover like my lover.

You got to have a baby like my baby.

There's no other baby—

and I don't mean maybe—

like my baby.

You got to have a lover

like my lover.

There's no other love like my lover.

Your Hot, Sexy Ass

I can't wait to make love to someone new

So I can stop thinking about you.

I kissed you everywhere

and all over you.

You wanted your wrists and ankles tied.

You had dark brown eyes

you hid in a mask behind.

Your hair was longish and black.

You had a black goatee

and you wore a black cock ring,

and it was one of a kind.

You wore a women's thong;

I think you went Brazilian as there

was there was no hair.

And oh, your hot, sexy ass.

You sang your sexy songs

with your eyes closed.

You were so handsome to me then

that way, and you still are to me now,

even though I know all the ladies show their breasts to you.

The way you look, so clean and clear,

in those days in every way.

I still think of you

near me and dear to me today.

I can see your back

as I laid my breasts down against it.

I kissed you everywhere and all over you.

But I still can't wait to meet someone new,

so I can stop thinking about you.

But I can remember your hot, sexy ass.

I Hate Him so Much

B

I hate him so much.

I hate him so much

Because he beat me up,

And now I hate him so much.

A

He uses me.

He hurts me.

He aggravates me.

He's a jerk.

He ruined my world,

And he's a creep.

It hurts down deep.

B

A

This is no love song;

This is a hate song.

This is what he deserves,

Fraying my nerves.

He makes me see

I need to be set free.

I don't like what I see.

B

A

He doesn't like the way I do it.

Got to bring me back to it.

He's a liar and a creep.

Burying myself deep.

I'm a nice girl,

But he ruined my world,

And it's the end.

Don't want to be his girlfriend.

B

I Love the Baddy Boy

A

I play all day with him

Cause he makes me feel okay within.

I can't stop wanting him,

Want to hop on his bike with him.

My family says to say goodbye,

And it makes me want to cry.

He makes me feel so high.

He's the dude who is always defending me

Because he always respects me.

B

I love the baddy, baddy boy.

I love the saddest, baddest boy.

I love the most inferior boy.

I love the most infurious boy.

C

Want to be his motorcycle mama.

Love to be his motorcycle mama.

Like the songs say,

Like the songs say,

Like the songs say,

I'll be the queen of his highway.

A

We will always be together,

In ecstasy forever.

We love each other exceedingly.

We will be together extremely.

He will always be my family.

D

He brings out the baddy, baddest girlie,

He brings out the baddy, saddest girlie

In me, in me, in me.

B

D

I bring out the goodie, goodie boy,

I bring out the goodie, goodie boy

In him, in him, in him.

C

D

I Was Born Crazy

I was born crazy,

and there's nothing I can do

because I was born crazy,

and I'll always be your fool.

I will always be a crazy fool for you

because I was born this way, you see.

But I've always been a child of God;

he loves me slow and mild.

Still, I was born crazy,

and there's nothing I can do.

Because I was born crazy,

and I'll always be your fool.

I play like a child with you,

and I'm nothing but your lady con.

But I am still a child of God.

He loves me anyway, you see.

You don't want me cause I'm crazy,

and there's nothing I can do.

Because I was born crazy,

and I'll always be your fool.

You're My Heaven

You're my heaven.

You make me feel like heaven.

I could only dream of heaven

until I found you,

and you became my heaven.

I always dreamt of heaven,

and you became my heaven.

I saw you there

in my white leather chair

with all your long blonde hair.

And there was no holding back.

You set me on the right track,

all positive and nothing bad.

I can't believe your kindness.

I can't believe your goodness.

I can hardly take your love.

You're so good,

and you're so kind,

and you're so wise.

I'll Kiss You a Million Times

B

Kiss me once, and hold me close,

and I'll kiss you a million times.

And I'll tell you

I'll never, ever leave you.

I'll never, ever leave you again.

A

We could be sweet

if our lips could meet.

Time could allow

taking out guitar vows.

If we became close,

our chests might explode.

Our affections might implode.

Our senses might lose control.

We will never grow old.

Our adorations flow.

Our affection is untold.

Tenderly we will unfold.

Our romance is palpitating spark.

Our eyes are kissing in the dark.

B

A

Our affair could never be over.

We're rolling in clover.

Our fondness is never-ending.

Our tender spirit's ascending

and never left contending.

We're excessively sexed wed

with my lips of painted red.

B

A

Now I'm all on my own,

and I'm left all alone

in my empty home.

Missing you, my darling, now bereaved.

Please help me grieve.

Losing you I could never foresee.

A life without you I can't believe.

I'll kiss you a million times.

B

Kiss me once, and hold me close,

and I'll kiss you a million times.

And I'll tell you

I'll never, ever leave you.

I'll never, ever leave you again.

A

We could be sweet

If our lips could meet.

Time could allow

Taking out guitar vows.

If we became close,

our chests might explode.

Our affections might implode.

Our senses might lose control.

We will never grow old.

Our adorations flow.

Our affection is untold.

Tenderly we will unfold.

Our romance is palpitating spark.

Our eyes are kissing in the dark.

B

A

Our affair could never be over.

We're rolling in clover.

Our fondness is never-ending.

Our tender spirit's ascending

and never left contending.

We're excessively sexed wed

with my lips of painted red.

B

A

Now I'm all on my own,

and I'm left all alone

in my empty home.

Missing you, my darling, now bereaved.

Please help me grieve.

Losing you I could never foresee.

A life without you I can't believe.

I'm Infatuated with You

B

I'm infatuated with you,

And it's so awesome

I'm infatuated with you,

And it's so much fun.

And you're the best one

Under the sun.

A

My infatuation with you is a development.

Our romance is an achievement.

I appreciate the enjoyment

That you bring into my life.

You're an amazement.

I'm looking for you at the bus stop.

You're right on the top.

I'm looking for you at the train.

I got you on the brain.

I'm looking for you at work.

Did you see me smirk?

Did you see that other girl's a jerk?

B

We'll be together, I know.

Crazy for you until the end.

Maybe not forever,

But we'll be great friends.

Please don't you escape me.

I got affection for you.

We can see this through;

For you I'll be true.

B

I gave you my all.

We could forever fall.

There will never be an end.

Our bodies could wed.

We'll be intimate

All over again.

B

I'm Loving You

I'm loving you for the thrills,

my lace, my frills.

I have your picture framed in lapis lazuli.

It reminds me of our past dreams.

The way we use to scheme our happenings

of diamond rings and things.

We could sit here and play all day.

That's what you used to say.

My love for you I hid

as if I were just a kid.

And I'll remember when I wake in the morning

and in my dreams at night,

I'll remember you when I wake in the morning

and in my dreams at night.

My love for you I hid

as if I were just a kid.

I'll remember you when I wake in the morning

and in my dreams at night.

My love for you I hid

as if I were just a kid.

And I'll remember you when I wake in the morning

and in my dreams at night.

I'm Infatuated with You

Chorus

I'm infatuated with you, and it's so awesome.

I'm infatuated with you, and it's so much fun.

And you're the best one

Under the sun.

A

My infatuation for you is a development.

Our romance is the achievement.

I appreciate the enjoyment

That you give me.

You're an amazement

I'm looking for you at the bus stop.

I got you right on top.

I'm looking for you at the train.

I got you on the brain.

I'm looking for you at work.

Did you see me smirk?

That other girl's a jerk?

B

A

We'll be together I know.

I'll be crazy for you

Until the end.

Maybe not forever,

But we'll be great friends.

Please don't escape me;

I got affection for you.

We can see it through

For you I'll be true

B

I gave for you my all.

We could forever fall.

There will be no end,

And if we should wed,

We'll make it happen

All over again.

Insanity

Refrain

My maddest and baddest

Has consequences of the saddest.

Verse 1

Can't feel your heat against my life.

Can't feel your hardness in the night.

When the owl turns its head and takes flight,

I'm missin' all our lovin',

Cuddlin' and huggin'.

Verse 2

You've been gone so long.

You see I'm not that strong.

My madness I can't weather.

My strength is like a feather.

My future I can't see,

Just an unfortunate destiny

Ending my big schemes.

Need you in my dreams.

The nightmare, now my future,

Is just a bleeding suture.

Refrain

Verse 3

You've come back to say goodbye.

You were never a waste of my time.

I will always miss you, my sweet.

Your sultry taste can't be beat.

None could ever compete.

I'll love you till the end.

See you round the bend,

When we rise in the end.

So sorry we can't be friends.

Refrain

Verse 4

Being your hookup

Was a big mistake.

Need you near me

And on the make.

Now my future without you awaits.

It Was a Busy Day Today

B

It was a busy, busy, busy, busy day today.

Such a busy, busy, busy, busy day today

Because I'm with you today,

So true to you today,

Never blue with you today

In any way today.

A

I want to make you mine today

Because you're so fine today.

I can see in your blue eyes today.

I can feel the warmth of you within.

Being without you is a sin.

With you I have a rush of adrenaline.

B

A

I'm with you and my devotion.

I'll stick with you through thick and thin.

You're like my Aladdin.

You send me in a tailspin.

You see, I'm very bashful.

You look so dishful.

B

A

On our date you were quite prompt.

We went on a big, bad romp.

Never met a man of such high quality.

You are my priority.

You're number one in the majority.

You're my devoted prodigy.

B

THE SHE DEVIL WITHIN

I got a she devil inside of me

She devil won't you please stop possessing me?

She devil jump outside of me

Won't you please stop possessing me?

You've made me sick and old before my time

You've made it so I haven't earned a dime

She devil keeps tempting me to sin

That young she devil within

She devils she won't win

She devil won't you please jump outside of me

She devil stop messing with me

She devil won't you please stop possessing me

She devil stop the little girl within

CHORUS

Jump out! Jump out! She devil! She devil! Jump out!

Jump out! She devil! She devil! Jump out!

REPEAT SONG AND CHORUS

STALKER

A

I'll remember you tomorrow

He told me when I was a girl

A night of sorrow

I rocked his world

A

It was m

y first lovin

It was the first coming

You needed me near you

I couldn't adhere to you

A

Why couldn't you see

I needed you to leave me be

I just didn't believe

I was all you could ever need

A

In the eyes of a stranger

I felt all the danger

You needed to leave me be

You said I needed to believe

A

You needed me close

You were so grandiose

I wanted to leave

But you had to have me

A

You said so direct

That I was a secret

Your love only hurt me

You had me up your sleeve

A

You just couldn't leave me alone

Ruining my happy home

You couldn't see

I needed you to leave me be

B

Stalker, Stalker

Midnight honker

What a talker

Midnight walker

Can't you see

I need you to leave me be?

I need to believe

That you will leave

Please, Please

Just leave me alone

All alone in my home

Please, Please

Just leave me be

Stalker, stalker

What a honker

Such a talker

Midnight walker

Please, please leave me be,

And set me free.

HE'S A CHEATER

He's a cheater

He's a mistreater

He's a deceiver

He's afraid of losing her

He sees other women on the side

And he won't tell nothing but lies

But he's never satisfied

He's reckless, selfish and mean

And other women that he sees

Well, he says that

"they don't mean a thing"

And his woman

she doesn't

suspect a thing

And she believes

that he's loyal

But he's nothing

like that at all

He's a cheater

He a mistreater

He's a deceived

And he's afraid of losing her

And he's sees

other women

on the side

And he can't tell

nothing but lies

And he's never satisfied

He's a cheater

He's a mistreater

He's a deceiver

INTIMATE STRANGER

A

It felt so strange

To be with a stranger

I haven't done it since I was young

I thought those days were gone forever

But there you were and it was all for fun

My intimate stranger, stranger, stranger

Laying naked in my bed

Then I watched you on YouTube and Facebook

And my intimate stranger he went straight to my head

To me you were my special someone

So dark, handsome, wise not dumb

Wasn't really sure I wanted you to come

Didn't know how special until you were gone

Now I sing this special song

B

You were my intimate stranger

Intimate stranger, stranger, stranger

You were the one

The one, one, one

My intimate stranger

Beautiful stranger, stranger, stranger

I sure missed you

When you were gone

Were gone, gone, gone

A

Now I've been all alone

And on my own

My beautiful one

We could have gotten something on

But honey, I'm just not that young

You are my soul

We stole the show

B

A

I didn't know how special you were

until you were gone

Now I sing my special song

To commemorate how strong

You were so fine

If only I made you mine

But boy you stole my heart away

So special in so many ways

B

A

Now over a year has passed

Time does fly fast

Even though I've tried

I can't make you mine

I've tried to be with others too

But they can't compare to you

I was so tender and true

B

You're the best that's happened

To me in so long my sweet

There is no one who could compete

I haven't met or could meet

Any one as tender or true

Don't know what's happened to you

But my feelings still true

My heart cries out my song for you

You were my intimate stranger

My intimate stranger

Intimate stranger, stranger, stranger

When you left, I lost my soul

That's when I got to know

The one man who stole the show

I'M LOVING YOU

I'm loving you for the thrills

my lace, my frills

I have your picture framed in lapis lazuli

It reminds me of our past dreams

The way we use to scheme our happenings

of diamond rings and things

We could sit here and play all day

that's what you use to say

My love for you I hid

as if I were just a kid

And I'll remember when I wake in the morning

and in my dreams at night

I'll remember you when I wake in the morning

and in my dreams at night

My love for you I hid

as if I were just a kid

I'll remember you when I wake in the morning

and in my dreams at night

My love for you I hid

as if I were just a kid

And I'll remember you when I wake in the morning

and in my dreams at night

MY FRIEND

He said he would always be my friend

He said he would be there till the end

But he's not as good a friend

As he once appeared to be, to me, to me

Now he's just someone that I love to hate

And he's just a little too late

He's not as nice as he looks

He's not as nice as he acts

And accidents always happen

When he's around

And that's no accident

He's a comedy king

But I know he's really mean

He doesn't act that way at all

And you can't tell that about him at all

Once you get to know his tricks

Then you'll know just where to stick it

He said he would always be my friend

He said he would be there till the end

But he's not as good a friend

As he once appeared to be to me, to me to me

MY MIND SOUL AND BODY

A

I adore the excitement you bring

to my whole entity

my mind, soul and body

I want you morning, noon

and night time too

I keep pictures of you on my phone

So, I can see you

when you're not home

A

Romance binds, us together as one

We're like a big ball exploding

As we explore each other's bodies

Romance binds, us together as one

I'll keep going back to you

Cause you're the one

I'm addicted to the excitement you bring

to my whole entity

my mind, soul and body

YOU HAVE A WALL UP

You have a wall up

that will never come down

It'll never come down

It'll never come down

No, no not for me

No, no not for me

You're nothing but a loving women man machine

You're so strong it hurts

You're so strong I weep

You're so strong I die

I needed you but you were never there

You were never there

You were never there

NO MEANS NO

A

He says no

He ignores me

No, no, no

He blocks me, no

He thinks of me no

He's unavailable

He thinks I'm wrong

And he's not there

And he's not here

Cause no means no

Love has faded fast

He's getting it somewhere else

B

And no means no

No, no, no

Because no means no

A

Love has faded fast

Cause no means no

He's getting it somewhere else

And no means no

No, no, no

Now I'm naked

Now I'm dumb

Now I'm plain

And now I'm flawed

Now I'm silent

And now I'm scared

B

Cause no means no

And he means no

No, no, no

Yes, no means no

No, No, No

DON'T WORRY BABY

C

And now the time has come

For us to say goodbye

My heart will break in a thousand parts

I feel like I could die

Without you, without you

I am nothing without you

B

Don't worry baby

Everything will be ok

I can't deny how you feel

And feeling it is so surreal

A

When you're away honey

I'll be waiting and praying

Everything will be ok

Come home soon

Because I'm so blue

You know how blue

I am without you

B

A

You're the only love

I've ever known

Take me back home

Away from the cold

The ice and the snow

I can't wait to see you

Some day if not today

Then what day?

Come what may

Can I see you?

If there was only a way

To see you soon

Someday, but anyway

B

REMEMBERING HIM

Making love in the green grass

Skinny dippin in the streams

Taking pictures of the mountains

And all the beauty that we see

But we didn't actually do those things

You told me to wear turquoise

And I wore it for you

Taking pictures in your studio

Body shots and close ups

We shot for you

My head, face and body

My legs and arms too

I moved them for you

I wore my pink bra and panties

Trying to look pretty for you

I was so happy

Under your lens

Every time, time again

We both suffered from depression

But we handled our transgressions

Shooting the day away

What else can I say

Making love in the green grass

Skinny dipping in the streams

But we didn't actually do those things

PRETENDING TO BE SOMEONE ELSE

B

It's not a good thing

It's a bad thing

Because we can't love each other this way

Pretending

Pretending

A

Pretending I don't like you so you like me

Pretending I don't want you so you'll want me

Could you like me the way I like you?

If you knew how much I liked you?

And could you want me the way I want you?

If you knew how much I want you?

But you don't like me because I like you

And you don't want me because I want you

And you lose and I lose

Pretending

Pretending

B

A

Pretending I don't like you so you like me

Pretending I don't want you so you'll want me

It's not a good thing

It's a bad thing

Because we can't love each other this way

Pretending

Pretending

I can't resist you

I got to have you

But you can't like me because I like you

And you can't want me because I want you

And we can't love each other this way

Pretending

Pretending

Pretending I don't like you so you'll like me

And I don't want you so you'll want me.

But we can't love each other this way

Pretending

Pretending

YOU'RE A LIAR

B

You're a liar

Oh, what a liar

My soul's ablaze

You got me crazed

You're a liar

Oh, what a liar

Such a liar, a liar

Oh, woe is me

Oh, woe is me

I don't deserve a man so mean

A man so keen

On hurting me

A

You're a player

A womanizer

My loyal soul's ablaze

You got me crazed

You keep up your double standards

You can't control my cheating tender desires

Mistreatment of the women you're scorned

And all the romances that you've torn

B

A

You're so passive

There's no communication

It means you're letting go of

A passion so strong

The passionate woman in me

The soul of me, in me

And those old times

I will keep and hold them near

To a soul once held so dear

Tender souls that we were once together

C

But you went and wounded

My passionate soul

Set it ablaze

You got me crazed

B

A

Once we were intwined together

Once my partner now my disdainer

Romance relations my broken hope

For a future together

You're a seducer

A Casanova,

A women cruiser

One we shared

A passion for each other

You it ablaze

You got me crazed

YOU'RE A LIAR

VERSION 1

You're a liar

Oh, what a liar

My soul's ablaze

You got me crazed

You're a liar

Oh, what a liar

Such a liar, a liar

Oh, woe is me

Oh, woe is me

I don't deserve

a man so mean

A man so keen

On hurting me

A

You're a player

A womanizer

My loyal soul's ablaze

You got me crazed

You keep up your double standards

You can't control my cheating tender desires

Mistreatment of the women you're scorned

And all the romances that you've torn

B

A

You're so passive

There's no communication

It means you're letting go of

A passion so strong

The passionate woman in me

The soul of me, in me

And those old times

I will keep and hold them near

To a soul once held so dear

Tender souls that we were once together

C

But you went and wounded

My passionate soul

Set it ablaze

You got me crazed

B

A

Once we were entwined together

Once my partner now my disdainer

Romance relations my broken hope

For a future together

You're a seducer

A Casanova,

A women cruiser

One we shared

A passion for each other

You it ablaze

You got me crazed

ROCHESTER IN THE SPRING

It's a beautiful day

And it's a fabulous place to live

There's a lovely breeze

And I feel like

I really want to give

Back to the people

Of this old place

The grass and trees

Are all green again

And the park is full

Of many children

My cat is happy

He's sitting and looking out the window

Now he's running around

And I wish I could go

Running around with him

Running laps around the trail system

There's a blue-sky abounding

And the blue ceiling

Makes me feel so abundant

My bad feelings are redundant

It's a magnificent day

It's a fabulous place to live

And it's a beautiful place

For me to love

SLAY THE DRAGON

He thinks I'm a bad and evil girl

Cause I send him in a whirl

In my dreams he's someone

I can't see

He wants the girl

I dare to be

Other girls think he's so sweet

And they think he'll make them complete

But he's playing a deadly game

I know I'll take all the blame

I'm a fair and beautiful maiden

And my troubles have all been laden

And he's a baddy and evil monster

His good looks and charms a caster

And totally makes me bluster

Now he's pinning me down

He's holding me down

He's forcing me down

PRE-CHORUS

Could you please kill this monster?

Would you please slay this dragon?

CHORUS

I'm looking for my hero

Yes, I'm looking for a champion

Want a man of courage

STAR 80

CHORUS

Star 80 Star 80

Star 80 Star 80

VERSE 1

The man you had was so mean

And just an insignificant thing

He did you wrong

And now your gone

He did you bad

It's so sad

But you're the most

Magnificent girl

Playboy ever had

Chorus

He treated you so mean

It really was a big bad scene

How unfortunate it was for you to go

You shouldn't have been treated so low

CHORUS

What a crime

And such a slime

And it's just a shame

Some people won't

Ever know your name

SLOW DANCING

A

I see you're slow dancing with someone else

I see you're slow dancing with someone new

And it makes me feel so blue

Because you know I've been untrue

Is that the best you can do?

When you know I've been untrue?

Yeah it makes me feel so blue

Because I know we are through

This is the end of me and you

A

Can we start all over again?

Start all over again?

Over again?

Over again?

Can I take it back my friend?

Take it back my friend?

My friend?

My friend?

A

I can't believe it's the end

Believe it's the end

It's the end?

The end

The end

Could we try it once again, my friend?

Try it once again?

Again, my friend

My friend

My friend

SONGS OF LOVE I SANG TO HIM

I sang songs of love I sang to him

A long time ago, all alone, when I waited for him to come

He had so many young and sexy women then

So many years of my life I lost to him and I will never have them back again

I learned how precious my life was without a man

I learned about love from the old songs I sang to him a long time ago

So many long nights I waited for him to come home

I sang songs of love I sang to him while I waited for him to come home

There were so many old romantic songs I sang to him a long time ago

When I waited for him to come home and I was all alone

I sang songs of love I sang to him, all alone, while I waited for him to come

So many old romantic old romantic songs I sang to him many years ago

When I waited for him to get back home

THE END IS NEAR

It's Armageddon

It's Armageddon

Oh, the end is coming

Oh, the end is coming

Yes, the end is near

And there'll be title waves

And there'll be hurricanes

There'll be earthquakes

And there'll be floods

It's Armageddon

It's Armageddon

It's Armageddon

Oh, the end is coming

Oh, the end is coming

Yes, the end is near

And there'll be racial injustices

And there'll be a pandemic

There'll be civil disobedience

And there'll be hatred

And there'll be anger

But we want peace

And we want love

It's Armageddon

It's Armageddon

It's Armageddon

Oh, the end is coming

Oh, the end is coming

Yes, the end is near

TO BIG FOR HIS BRITCHES

CHORUS

His ego's taller than the Empire State

He thinks he's so great

His ego is bigger than the sky up above

And he's looking for love

BRIDGE

And you know

Yes, I know

Yes, I know

POST CHORUS

He's getting too big for his britches

And all of his riches

He's getting much too big for his britches

And all of his riches

Yes, he's getting too big for his britches

He's much too big for his britches

VERSE 1

Maybe he's got a drinking problem?

Cause he acts so solemn

Maybe he's on drugs?

He hangs with thugs

I know what he does

He won't be not open

He's not copen

He leads a secret life

Free from strife

CHORUS

POST CHORUS

He's very low key

Not so free

He doesn't want anyone

To find out

What he does

I know this

Just because

He wants protection

It's a blessing

I'm not messing

He's headed in the wrong direction

CHORUS

POST CHORUS

VERSE 3

He leads a secret life

Free from strife

He's very low key

He won't be so free

He doesn't want anyone

To find out

Just what he does

Did you catch his buzz?

What he does here stays here

He plays by ear

He's ashamed of his sexuality

Not good for his masculinity

He's quite informal

By today's standards

He's quite normal

He keeps me guessing

And I'm confessing

He's not messing

And it's really a blessing

CHORUS

WE MUST IMPROVE THE BUST

Verse 1

I saw you looking at your favorite magazine

Couldn't help but notice what you were seeing

You want to see my cleavage?

Want to show you my lustievage

CHORUS

We got to put up

A good front

We must, we must

We must improve the bust

The bigger the better

The tighter the sweater

We must improve the bust

Verse 2

Saw you looking at your favorite magazine

Couldn't help but notice what you were seeing

I want to look that good

I hope, I'm knocking on wood

My beasts are sculpted of perfection

Don't want them sagging in the wrong direction

I need some protection

I can see them in my reflection

There good looks are a projection

My boobs re something you adore

These knockers weren't here before

Now I starting to mature

Do you know what these are for?

I don't want to be a bore

I don't want to be your whore

CHORUS

Can we settle this infraction?

I didn't see your reaction

I want to look my best

Prettiest chest in the Midwest

You really are straightforward

Putting my best foot forward

Want to be someone you adore

I can't be your warlord

CHORUS

CHORUS

YOU'RE A LIAR

(Version 2)

B

You're a liar

Oh, what a liar

My hearts ablaze

You got me crazed

Oh, what a liar

Keep on lying

About me baby

Oh, woe is me

Oh, woe is me

I don't deserve

A man so mean

And a man so keen

On hurting me

A

You're a controller

A womanizer

My tender soul

Is all ablaze

You got me crazed

You're so passive

There's no communication

Means you're letting go and

Tenderly I'm so strong

The spark in me

Oh, woe is me

A

And those memories

I will keep

And hold them near

To a soul once

Held so dear

Tenderly we shared together

But you went and torched

My tender soul

Set it all ablaze

You got me crazed

B

A

Once my lover

Now my hater

Love hate relations

And my broken spirit

Mistreatment and all the women you've scorned

And all the tender souls

Of the girls

That you've torn

A

You're so passive

No communication

Means you're letting go

Of a love so strong

The love of me

Oh, woe is me

And those memories

I will keep

And hold them near

Of a tender dance

Once held so dear

A tender dance we once shared together

A

But you went and torched

My tender soul

Set it ablaze

You got me crazed

You were once my lover

You're now my hater

Love hate relations

And a broken soul

B

ABOUT THE AUTHOR

JoAnn Logan Rathje is originally from Chicago, Illinois, and now resides in St. Paul, Minnesota. She was a hospitality model and photography model. She worked at McCormick Place. She worked at Marshall Field and Company, Lord and Taylor Fine Jewelers, Gucci, Bonwit Teller, and The Chicago Theatre. She attended Roosevelt University, the Chicago Conservatory of Music, Chicago Musical College, Harold Washington College, Chicago College of Commerce, McDaniel's School, Ray College of Design, and the Academy of Art University.

Printed in the United States
by Baker & Taylor Publisher Services

Printed in the United States
by Baker & Taylor Publisher Services